Business Expertise
WINNING OVER THE CUT-THROAT COMPETITION

Prriya Kaur

Copyright © 2020 Prriya Success Academy

All rights reserved.

ISBN: **978-1-65-254411-1**

"Nobody outside of your business would give you the answers. The answer to long term success lies within."

- Prriya Kaur

CONTENTS

   Acknowledgments   i

1   Introduction   Pg 1

2   Principle 1   Pg 4

3   Principle 2   Pg 38

4   Principle 3   Pg 54

5   Principle 4   Pg 58

6   Principle 5   Pg 63

7   Principle 6   Pg 74

8   Principle 7   Pg 88

9   References   Pg 98

Disclaimer:

Before you invest here in the form of time, efforts or money, be sure to carefully consider the investment objectives, expenses involved, possible risks and probability of changes. All investment involved may be at risk including loss of principal investment. Past performance does not guarantee future success and results. The parties contributing to this product are not registered/licensed investment advisors. Their opinions and comments are their own. There are not meant to be taken as investment recommendations and advice. Additionally, their opinions and comments do not reflect the opinions of, nor should they be attributed to, the copyright holder.

The plans drew are simply the results of huge research done in this field and are not just our personal recommendations. We only deliver our teachings around the world which are helpful to people which is clear from the results of our research. We advise you to use highest and due diligence before you invest money in any course.

Dear Achievers:

Welcome to **Business Expertise**, this program is completely designed to help your business grow more regardless of the existing economic conditions. The reality is, there are certain patterns that cause people to succeed in life and business. In addition, you must learn how to apply the principles and strategies which have worked for others and thus commit yourself to follow the necessary footsteps.

The focus of this program is how to maximize the impact, how to optimize and grow profitability of your enterprise, complete a combination of skills, learning from others and direct experience. We will together find out and seek out the core tipping points that can make the biggest difference in your business in the shortest time.

By the time you leave, you will understand what your customers really want and how to meet their needs in the most efficient ways possible. You will know what you really want out of your business as well as have the means to attain it.

You will understand the psychology of your customers, your employees and yourself. You will have more skills and be adaptable in your business as you will be able to see more opportunities that your competitors will miss out. You will gain a sense of confidence and power that will set you up to win.

Let's continue the journey and, as always, remember to live with passion and never ever give up until you achieve the results which you want.

INTRODUCTION

(Creating a world-class business)

"Good business leaders create a vision, articulate the vision, passionately own the vision, and relentlessly drive it to completion."

- JACK WELCH

Create a massive transformation in your business

What is the single main part that is going to create a massive transformation in your business and creating Business Breakthroughs and allow you both, the joy you reach in the process as well as increase your profit?

Business Expertise core purpose: Creating breakthrough

Have you thought about what is a breakthrough? It is a moment in time when you take a decision, create a new experience, create new truth, develop a new understanding, and learn that life is never the same again as a result.

Breakthroughs come from mastering the small things that make the biggest difference

Sometimes, it is a blind spot that suddenly opens up for you. For others, it is seeing problems they did not even know existed and being able to tackle them head-on. Or a new decision about who your primary customer needs to be. For some, it is a newfound ability to negotiate effectively and for others it is understanding the true margins of their business for the first time.
You are unable to change something if you are not aware of it. But once you have that awareness, one distinction can change the entire game.

Our Main Focus:

How you can maximize and optimize your profitability and the impact of your business, regardless of the external environment and the marketplace you are in?

Notes:

PRINCIPLE 1

BUILD A SUCCESSFUL BUSINESS PLAN

(Find out your Business Life cycle where you really are and create an effective Business Plan)

"All you need is the road map and the courage to press on to your destination"

- EARL NIGHTINGALE

2.1 Five rules you must be perfect in:

RULE 1: What business are you really in?

For creating a sustainable system that allows you to consistently increase the quality of the lives of the people you serve and your own life, ultimately, your business must generate fulfilment and freedom. The challenge is that most people get caught up in the journey instead of the outcome.

RULE 2: What is the purpose of the enterprise?

Create a value system in order to change the quality of life for your customers. For example, you must serve your clients in a totally unique and special way and consistently give them what they need and want.

RULE 3: How to make profit?

Always remember, if you make profit but fail meeting the customer's needs, you would not be able to survive in business for a long-term.

RULE 4: What makes a business grow?

Consistently adding more value than anyone else is adding in the market leads to a constant growth in business. The secret is that you must fall in love with your customers and not your products.

RULE 5: What is the difference between a job and a business?

If your business is organized to meet your needs instead of the needs of your customers, you ultimately have a job and not a business. You must differentiate between the purpose of the business and your own personal objectives like what you want to get out of the business.

EXERCISE:

1) What business are you really in?

_____
_____
_____
_____
_____
_____
_____

2) How is your business going?

_____
_____
_____
_____
_____
_____
_____

3) What is the gap between where you want to be and where you are now?

_____
_____
_____
_____
_____

4) What does the business need now to grow?

_____
_____
_____
_____
_____
_____

5) What business do you need to be in to have an extremely competitive advantage?

_____
_____
_____
_____
_____
_____

2.2 Defining your ultimate vision: What you want from your business.

Have you thought about what makes the business work and why it gives you the fuel to persevere through all the ups and downs?

Well, you may have inevitably experienced over the years – any business can work if the people or the person behind it has intensity and passion and if they can be flexible enough and adjust when necessary. Most of the times, why the business you got in is not why you are not in it today. However, when you do not align your compelling reasons for being in business, as a result, you are not going to maximize it.

As we know, business takes a lot of energy when you are to make it truly successful from the ground up or even when you are going to buy the business and turn it around or take it to another level. The energy will burn you physically and emotionally and make you feel exhausted and so on. But you have to have a reason and vision of something you are truly passionate about, especially where you are serving others more than yourself. This gives you energy and keeps you going regardless of any obstacles you hit along the way.

EXERCISE:

1) Why did you get in this business originally?

_____
_____
_____
_____
_____

2) Why are you in it now?

_____
_____
_____
_____
_____

3) What do you need to get from this business in the long-term?

_____
_____
_____
_____
_____

2.3 The 3 gifts of service and bringing them in line with your true nature:

a) Are you a skilled producer?

b) Are you a manager or a leader?

c) Are you an entrepreneur?

1. Skilled producers who have extraordinary talent, consistently meet the needs of the community they serve in a sustainable way.

2. A manager has management skills, but some do not have leadership skills. You must find leaders to cultivate. A leader who has skills to manage and meet the needs of skilled producers consistently meets the needs of the community in a sustainable way.

3. An entrepreneur must have skills and work with managers and leaders to create and build a system that consistently empowers skilled producers to meet the needs of the community they serve in a sustainable way. They could take risk and be able to personally weigh the economic and emotional difficulties of the business and be willing to take major personal risks and be a creator and keeper of a vision.

EXERCISE:

1) Who are you?
_____
_____
_____
_____
_____
_____

2) What do you need to learn?
_____
_____
_____
_____
_____
_____

3) Who do you need to get rid of in your business?
_____
_____
_____
_____
_____
_____

4) Who are your current clients?

_____
_____
_____
_____
_____
_____

5) Who do your clients need to be?

_____
_____
_____
_____
_____
_____

6) What do your clients need?

_____
_____
_____
_____
_____
_____

7) What are your clients going to need?

_____
_____
_____
_____
_____
_____

2.4 KNOWING THE ROAD AHEAD – WHAT SEASON ARE YOU IN

To succeed, it is vital to do the right thing at the right time, especially in business. As we enter a new season of history, the most important thing any of us can do is to understand where we are now, to find the current opportunities and ultimately to create a compelling and strategic vision for our future.

"Knowledge is static; wisdom is active and moves knowledge, making it effective." - Dr Will Mayo

2.5 Five essential areas of focus:

There are 5 fundamental areas of focus. Each stage of business life cycle requires a fundamental shift in focus in five areas. They are:

1) GOALS:
What is the focus and goal of the organization?

2) MANAGEMENT STYLE AND STRUCTURE:
What is the structure of decision-making?
Who has the responsibility and authority?

3) GROWTH OR DECLINE OF REVENUES AND PROFITS:
What is your cash position?
How much are your revenues and profits?

4) TYPE OF PROBLEMS:
At each life cycle, there are different types of problems that need to be solved. What problems do you need to anticipate? Which problems do you need to ignore? Which problems do you need to anticipate?

5) TYPES OF REWARDS:
Which reward systems will destroy you at each level?
What is the reward system that is needed to get to the next level?

2.6 Ten stages of the life cycle of a business:

STAGE 1 - BIRTH
The moment you take on risk
Work to meet own needs
Manage yourself

STAGE 2 - INFANCY
A Race for survival
Hire a person
You are running the business
Focus= production
Cash flow= significant challenge

STAGE 3 - TODDLER
Management by crisis
Business- walks and talks, on its own
Have begun to build a management team
Business still relies on you for all core decisions
Everything= accelerated
Cash flow still a concern

STAGE 4 - TEENAGER

The crisis created by management

Develop a professional team to manage business

Cash flow no longer a challenge

Growth- focus, innovation= rampant

More means better

Go- go leaders do not attend the meeting

You become overconfident

Trouble –imminent

STAGE 5 – YOUNG ADULT

Beginning to anticipate future

Make more committed choices

Limit what you focus on

Start a focus on system

Redefine what = success in long term settles down and get serious

STAGE 6 – ZONE OF MAXIMIZATION AND MATURITY

Reaping the reward

Develop a system for managing a business that allows

you to consistently meet the needs of the community

you serve and yourself in a sustainable way

Business- ran by a management team
An organization knows who it is, who it is not and
What it will do in the future
Sales and profits are growing

STAGE 7 – MIDLIFE EVALUATION

things begin to break down

entropy has begun

you evaluate whether to rejuvenate or to continue to age.

You must innovate, or you begin to die

STAGE 8 - AGEING

Breakdown begins to accelerate

State of denial – problems are not that big

Focus= how you are the victim

You begin to attack or blame

Talented people begin to leave

STAGE 9 - INSTITUTIONALIZATION

The organization is kept alive artificially through subsidization.

Kept alive by system rules and policies but there is

no innovation or focus on serving the needs of the community
STAGE 10 - DEATH
Vision = no longer sustainable
No people to support it

2.7 Ten stages of the lifecycle of a business (Thorough study):

STAGE 1 – BIRTH: STAGE OF CERTAINTY: (You must have certainty at this stage or you should not start the business)	
The moment you start; you take on a significant personal risk. Most people at this stage work to meet their own needs and hence, have a job and not a business. You end up primarily managing yourself. To succeed, you need to think of the needs of the business as something different from your own needs	

STAGE 2 – NEW BORN AND INFANT:	

STAGE OF UNCERTAINTY	In this stage, your business has now entered in a race for survival, where you can hire a person to handle the increased workload that resulted from the successful birth of your business. You are at the stage where you have independent managers but not the organized team and you are really running the business. Your focus is almost entirely on production and cash flow is a significant challenge.
GOAL	To grow and survive
MANAGEMENT STYLE	At this stage, you are an army of one.
GROWTH AND DECLINE	Revenues need to grow quickly because they are going to be spent.

PROBLEMS	a) Does not know the difference between revenue and profits b) Cash flow c) No system and lack of accounting
REWARDS	Very little rewards can be offered at this stage. The owner works for free and either inspires others to give their time or pays small salaries or stipends.

STAGE 3: TODDLER
(MANAGEMENT BY CRISIS)

STAGE OF BOTH UNCERTAINTY AND CERTAINTY	This stage is where business starts to talk and to walk on its own. You have started to build your team with leaders and management team, but you still maintain an absolute control in your hand. Your management team has started to work together. However, they still depend on your core decisions. Everything accelerates at this stage of development. Still, cash flow is a concern, but you are making significant progress and make refined distinctions.
GOAL	To grow, survive and begin to build a company.
MANAGEMENT STYLE	At this stage, the owner must be able to manage the team and still have absolute control and the management team begins to form and work together, but the owner still has all the authority and is relied upon for all the core decisions, even if others are made responsible.

GROWTH AND DECLINE	The income must rise because revenues are used as when are profits.
PROBLEMS	Lack of accounting and no system. The business can talk and walk, so there are others that can make decisions and create problems.
REWARDS	There is excitement and pride in being a part of something with a compelling future.

STAGE 4: TEENAGER (CRISIS BY MANAGEMENT)	

STAGE OF TOTAL CERTAINTY:	At this stage the cash flow is no longer a challenge. Growth is your primary focus and innovation is rampant. You start to develop a professional team to manage the business. You want to do everything and you think you can do it. You incorrectly think more means better and you become overconfident. You do not attend meetings and there is a lack of accountability. Systems are weak. Trouble looms on the horizons and your business is organized around people's tasks.
GOAL	At this stage, focus is on growth and income. Growth in innovation in both service and products and sometimes even multiple companies. Increase creativity, sales and continuous entrepreneurship.
MANAGEMENT STYLE	Your professional management team has the responsibility, but the core authority and the structure of decision is still through the owner.

GROWTH AND DECLINE	In the early stages, cash grows but in later stages it begins to decline rapidly because it no longer covers the basis of the business and sales expand but profit is unknown and non-existent.
PROBLEMS	Overconfidence makes the decisions, but it can kill or morally wound the business. Lack of accountability, failure to attend meetings and accounting is sales-focused versus profit-focused. Everything is seen as an opportunity, so problems are not solved on a timely basis. Lack of system with risks taken without the fundamental understanding of the down side.
REWARDS	Normally in the form of commission and revenues, it is based upon increased sales, which ultimately reinforces people to sell at all costs without economic measurement and without quality systems. It can lead to the demise of the organization.

STAGE 5: YOUNG ADULT (THE RE-BIRTH)

STAGE OF RE-ESTABLISHING CERTAINTY	At this stage, you start to redefine what equals success in the long-term. You represent a rebirth of the identity where you begin to settle down and get serious. You create a new and different identity as an adult. But you start to limit what you focus on – you start to mature

	and create an absolute focus on the systems that will shape the aspects of your life and business. You are beginning to anticipate the future and make more committed choices.
GOALS	The focus is on building the systems and most importantly on increasing profits versus income and control measurements to anticipate the future, in order to make more committed and educated choices. The goal is to cut the waste.
MANAGEMENT STYLE	The structure of decision-making no longer runs through the founder, although they still retain the ability to override but rarely do. The management team is made up of professional managers who have fought the war before. They have the responsibility, authority and ability to say "No".
GROWTH AND DECLINE	Cash position starts to build back. The profits expand, and incomes drop.
PROBLEMS	Psychological difficulties for the founders and creators in the company because the entrepreneur's nature is to create new things, and this can throw the organization back into the teenager stage or destroy it. Things are now going into a controlled measurement mode because deciding what not to do can lead to inner conflicts of teams which used to have the freedom or the answer "Yes" to everything.
REWARDS	Profits are increasing, individual behavior moves in the direction of these new rewards and so too, the corporate.

STAGE 6: ZONE OF MAXIMIZATION AND MATURITY

STAGE OF CERTAINTY	At this stage, the value is on sustainable growth. The organization knows what they will do in the future, who they are and who they are not. There is a predictable excellence. Sales and profits are growing. There are clear goals and they are controlled and nurtured. This is a time of reward and great certainty. The business is no longer run by the wishes of one person – it is led by a message, values, and a reason for being.
GOAL	This stage is building a professional team that makes all the decisions to serve customers at the highest level, both internally and externally. Also, this stage's goals are to create an organization that has a vision, brings it to the world and raises revenue and profits.
MANAGEMENT STYLE	The management team has the responsibility and authority is structured and is not based on the owner but based on what's needed and what's right. Also, the professional team must be an expert in innovation, creation and entrepreneurship.
GROWTH AND DECLINE	Cash position is strong with improved incomes and profits.
PROBLEMS	Owners tend to develop interests with other business interests both spiritually and in their relationships. People begin to lower their intensity and System Bureaucracy can start to be created. Costs are not managed as well. Lack of order begins.
REWARDS	Rewards are related, specifically to the behavior needed, managers and leaders are tied to growth in both revenue and profits and salespeople get revenue and/or profit numbers.

STAGE 7: MIDLIFE EVALUATION (THE TRANSITION)

STAGE OF UNCERTAINTY	At this stage, your business becomes old and you find that what worked before doesn't work anymore. You must add innovation, remove some control and add more creativity. Otherwise, your business begins to die and things begin to deteriorate and fall apart. During this stage, you begin to question your strategy and start formulating an exit strategy.
GOAL	The focus is on creating innovation to meet customers' needs in new ways. Renew systems and control systems. Failure to do this accelerates ageing.
MANAGEMENT STYLE	You have to bring in a new professional team with new creativity for some new blood and the re-engagement of the creator/visionary/owner.
GROWTH AND DECLINE	Revenues start to drop and as do sales but profits may hold up for a little bit longer because the systems are strong enough to extract value.
PROBLEMS	a) The owner/visionary or original stake-holder may have left the business. b) Blaming versus resolving. c) Do not have the same level of commitment to the vision or the business because Some of the original team may age and be at a different stage of life. d) Even customers are taken for granted.
REWARDS:	At this stage, they need to be rewarded for innovation.

STAGE 8: AGING
(THE BREAK DOWN)

STAGE OF UNCERTAINTY	When you fail to rebuild, the breakdown begins to accelerate and this blame-frame freezes the organization and talented people begin to leave. But you put yourself in a state of denial that the problems aren't that big. Next, you focus on how you're the victim of something or someone and you begin to attack.
GOAL	Try to survive and not be responsible for trying to blame someone.
MANAGEMENT STYLE	An aged team that fights for authority, territory and positioning, they lay blame rather than taking responsibility and/or transforming.
GROWTH AND DECLINE	Sales and profits are dropping rapidly.
PROBLEMS	Entropy is in full swing. Process problems, systems breakdown, customer problems and people problems. Blame freezes the organization, victimization and attack becomes the basis of the culture and destroys the ability to rebuild the organization.
REWARDS	The ultimate is you do not get to be paid today.

STAGE 9: INSTITUTIONALIZATION

STAGE OF UNCERTAINTY	When the organization would be dead but is kept alive on life-support through nationalization or subsidization. There could be little purpose left but the only things keeping you alive are the systems, policies, procedures and rules. There is no focus on serving the needs of the community and no focus on innovation. There is no longer any sense of control.
GOAL	You can keep it alive for more weeks, months, or years.
MANAGEMENT STYLE	The focus is on the preservation of what it was.
GROWTH AND DECLINE	Both revenues and sales are dropping rapidly.
PROBLEMS	Loss of customers, key accounts and key people. Process breakdown. Margins disappear. Blaming versus resolving. Every type of problem occurs. System breaks down.

STAGE 10: DEATH

NOTES:

2.8 EXAMPLE FOR THE CYCLE OF AN ORGANIZATION:

2.8.1 EXAMPLE 1: KINKO'S COMPANY STORY

1) BIRTH (1969):

The concept of Kinko's began when Paul Orfalea, a University of Southern California student, noticed the copy machine in the school's library and wanted to bring this technology to more students. He borrowed $5,000 from a local bank and rented a 100-square-foot space next to a hamburger stand at University of California, Santa Barbara, renting one Xerox copier.

2) INFANCY (1970):

In the first year of business, Kinko's charged $0.04 per page. Orfalea was selling pens, paper and other items right out of his backpack. From his sales, he was making $2,000/day while still in school.

3) TODDLERS (EARLY 1970's):

After the first few years, with no money or credit to expand, Paul got resourceful. He found an owner and operating partners to invest and kept a controlling interest.

4) TEENAGER (EARLY 1980's):

In 1985, Kinko's opened its first 24-hour copy retail store in Chicago, Illinois. Three years later, it had expanded to 200 locations with annual sales of $54 million.

5) YOUNG ADULT (1989):

In 1989, Orfalea faced a copyright infringement lawsuit that cost him years of distraction and $1.9 million.

6) THE ZONE (MID 1990's):

In 1995, Kinko's moved away from the college market and went after the corporate and small business industries. By this time, their retail stores were four times larger and one year later, they created an award-winning website.

7) MID-LIFE (MID 2000's):

Once Orfalea left the business and FedEx took over, the innovation was lost.

8) AGING (2008):

By 2008, Kinko's sales were down by 56%.

2.8.2 EXAMPLE 2: APPLE'S COMPANY STORY

1) BIRTH (1976):

Apple was established in 1976 by Steve Jobs and Steve Wozniak in the garage of Job's parents' house. Jobs had to sell his VW bus to finance the Apple I.

2) INFANCY (1976):

The Apple I was sold for $666.66 in July of 1976.

3) TODDLER (1983):

After five years of development, the Apple Lisa was released in 1983 as the first personal computer sold with a graphical user interface.

4) TEENAGER (1984):

In 1984, Apple debuted its new line of Macintosh computers, geared towards professionals, during a Superbowl commercial, considered to be the defining moment for Apple's brand.

5) YOUNG ADULT (1985):

After an internal power struggle between Jobs and new CEO John Sculley, Jobs resigned.

6) THE ZONE (EARLY 1990's):

The Macintosh continued to grow as Apple, added a new product line - the laptop. The late 1980's through the early 1990's were their first "Golden Age". But the 1990's brought struggle as Windows was first introduced and IBM surpassed the Mac in sales.

7) MIDLIFE (1997):

The company jumped back up to mid-life in 1997 when Apple brought back Jobs to turn the company around. He began the revitalization of Apple's brand and product line, as well as announced a partnership with Microsoft.

8) AGING (1995-1996):

There are major layoffs at Apple. Many software developers stopped building for Apple.

How Do You MAKE A COMPANY YOUNG AGAIN?

(Bring back the entrepreneurship)

1998: The first iMac.

2009: The evolved iMac 5.

2001 - Present: The most successful music distribution device in history: the iPod.

2009: The evolved iMac 5.

2007: The first iPhone.

2010: The first iPad.

There are the 7 triggers of crisis in the business:

1. Company Products
2. Change Culture
3. Change Economy
4. Change customers' Lives
5. Changes in Employees' Lives
6. Change your Life Stage
7. Change in Competition
   (make good perception)

2.9 EXERCISE: WHERE ARE YOU NOW?

1) Where are you in the life cycle of your business? Which stage is your organization currently experiencing? Why?

_____
_____
_____
_____
_____
_____
_____

2) Where is the life cycle of your industry? What stage of life is the industry you are part of experiencing? Why?

_____
_____
_____
_____
_____
_____
_____

3) Where is the economy? What life cycle is the economy in?

_____
_____
_____
_____
_____

4) Where are you personally? What life cycle are you experiencing as an individual working in your business?

_____
_____
_____
_____
_____
_____
_____

5) Where is your core team? What life cycle are they experiencing in your business?

_____
_____
_____
_____
_____
_____
_____

6) Where is your business in the seasons of change?

_____
_____
_____
_____
_____
_____

7) How do you need to prepare for the next season?

_____
_____
_____
_____
_____
_____
_____

Notes:

PRINCIPLE 2

POWERFUL LEADERSHIP FOR EXPLOSIVE GROWTH

"My job as a leader is to make sure everybody in the company has great opportunities, and that they feel they're having a meaningful impact."

- LARRY PAGE

3.1 Introduction:

Whether you have a multi-million-dollar industry, or you have a small company just getting started, there is a lasting change in business that comes down to individuals. All breakthroughs in business stem from someone's innovative ideas and insights. And what changes your actions are shifts in psychology and emotion. Thus, the key to changing your business is changing yourself.

3.2 Your Wish-List:

1) What transformations, changes and shifts would you like to see in your business?

_____
_____
_____
_____
_____
_____
_____

2) What would you like to learn new skills and to be master of it?

_____
_____
_____
_____
_____
_____
_____

3) What kind of challenges are you facing in your business?

_____
_____
_____
_____
_____
_____

4) What goals do you want to achieve?

_____
_____
_____
_____
_____
_____

5) Why do you want to make these changes in your business?

_____
_____
_____
_____
_____
_____

6) When you make these changes in your business, what would it mean?

_____
_____
_____
_____
_____
_____
_____
_____

7) Have you thought about it? What would be its worth to you (physically, emotionally, and financially)?

_____
_____
_____
_____
_____
_____
_____
_____

3.3 Managing Your State:

You already know that **your state** influences everything that you do. Most people know what to do, however, they do not perform it because of their state. For example, if you are consumed with fear, all of the decisions you make from that state will be guarded and lacking all your potentials. Or, when you are running from a place of greed, you are likely to start taking risks that you haven't fully thought over, which will create challenges for you in a different way. Thus, it is **imperative to know** what is influencing you as a leader.

3.4 Two forces that influence our decisions:

1. STATE	Moment to moment
2. BLUEPRINT	Long-term

3.5 The Power of Decisions:

Our decisions affect every area of our lives. Decision-making is the force that shapes all aspects of your personal and professional life. Making better decisions means living a better life. In fact, you can look back at your life and see where a key decision made several years ago projected a path that has led you to a dramatically different life. But how can we develop the habit of making great decisions? There is one of the key secrets to success: getting better at decision making.

THE 3 DECISIONS WE MAKE EVERY MOMENT

1. What should I focus on?

2. What does this mean?

3. What should I do?

Decision-making is your power.

1. What was one of the worst decisions you ever made?
_____
_____
_____
_____

What did you learn from it?
_____
_____
_____
_____

2. Mention one of the greatest successes of your business career.
_____
_____
_____
_____

What did you learn from it?
_____
_____
_____
_____

Two Decisions – One Small, One Big.

1. Which is a small decision that you can make right now that will change your business?

_____
_____
_____
_____

2. Which is a tough decision that will make a sizable improvement in your business?

_____
_____
_____
_____

3. What will you do to act on these decisions?

_____
_____
_____
_____

4. How will they change your business?

_____
_____
_____
_____

NOTES:

3.6 Training Effect:

In order to create the change, you desire, you need to understand how people learn and integrate new skills. Then only you can set yourself and your team to win by creating a training system that anticipates the unavoidable plateaus in the process. This program brings all employees to a higher level so they all have similar skills and knowledge. Also, you can bring your distinctions back to your team to start taking your company to a new level.

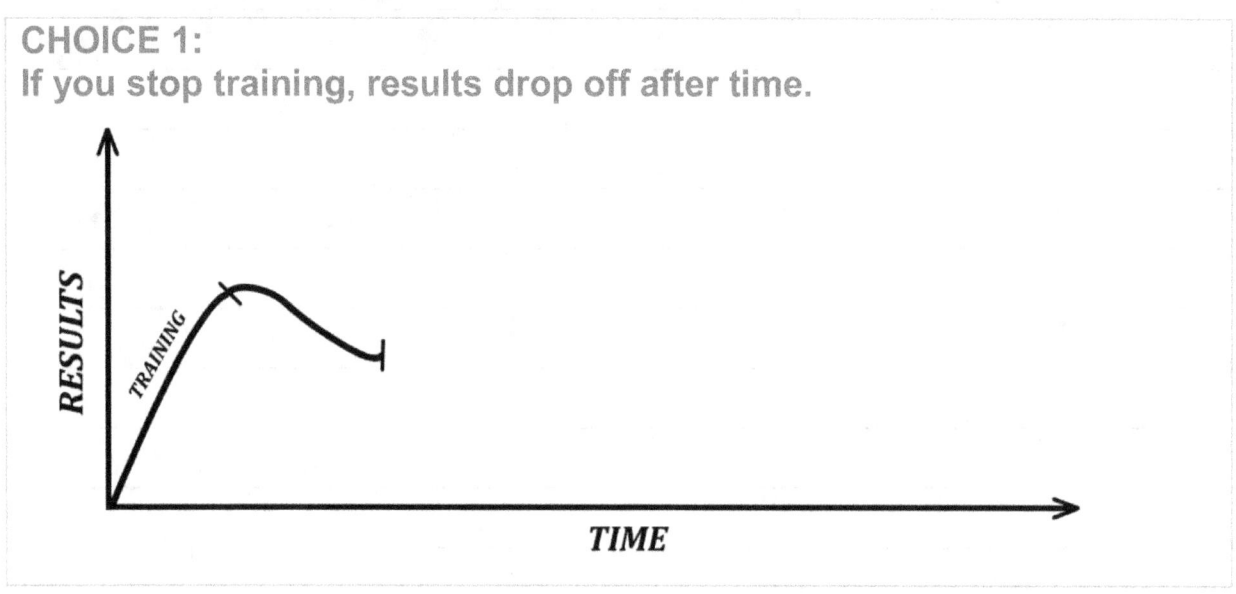

CHOICE 1:
If you stop training, results drop off after time.

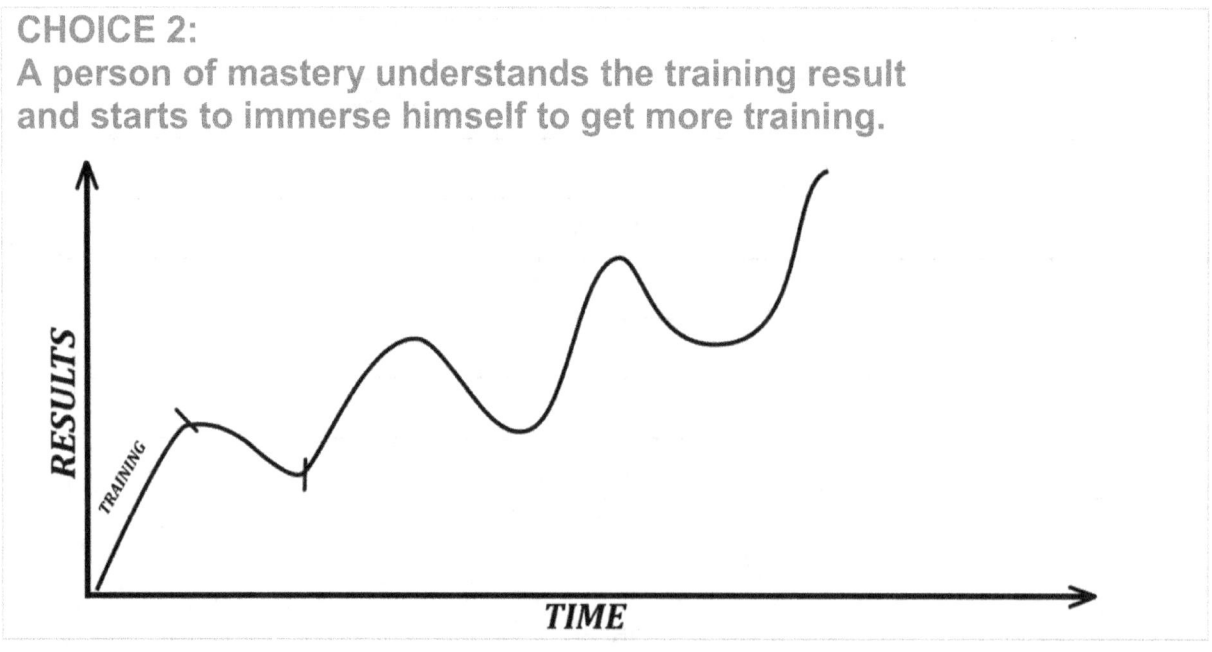

CHOICE 2:
A person of mastery understands the training result and starts to immerse himself to get more training.

3.7 Knowing the Road Ahead:

ANTICIPATION – An Unstoppable Power:

In life and business when you can expect what is coming, you can overcome any obstacle placed in your path. You can see the problems and that put you in a place of power. From this point of view, you can take actions to plan that will drive you forward and you can create the solutions, rather than reacting and getting stuck or hung up on common issues.

Remember, success leaves clues. The best way to foresee potential problems is to study and model those who have already been down the path you are taking. When you master this concept, a whole new world of possibilities opens for you.

Maximizing Resources – How Leaders Succeed:

Why do people not achieve their goals? Most people will tell you that they failed because they were lacking a resource (time, money, people, experience, etc.). But the truth is that there is always a way out. A successful leader is a person who maximizes his resources. Even in the most inconvenient situations, this is a person who can always find a solution. Thus, the ultimate resource is resourcefulness and the corresponding emotion needed to drive your passion to follow through no matter what. Then, once you start to expect challenges, the next key is to be a master at finding solutions.

3.8 Powerful Leadership (The Secret to Explosive Growth):

DECISION AND ACTIONS	BY WHEN	LEVERAGE AND WHY	RESOURCES

Notes:

3.9 THREE WAYS TO GROW YOUR BUSINESS (How to Create Regular Growth Now):

According to Jay Abraham, the only three ways to grow any business can be categorized as follows:

1. Increase the number of customers (clients).
2. Increase the average transaction value.
3. Increase the frequency of repurchases - get more residual value out of each customer.

SMALL COMPANY EXAMPLE:

Current # of Customers 1.000 X	Increase the average £ per Sale 100 X	Increase the repurchase frequency 2	Total £200.000
10 % increase	10 % increase	10 % increase	33.1%
20% increase	20 increase	20 %increase	72.8 %
33 % increase	25% increase	50 %increase	150%

If your business is a one-time sale, you may want to instead count the number of referrals you get and convert the sale or consider adding an ongoing service to sell that can increase your frequency.

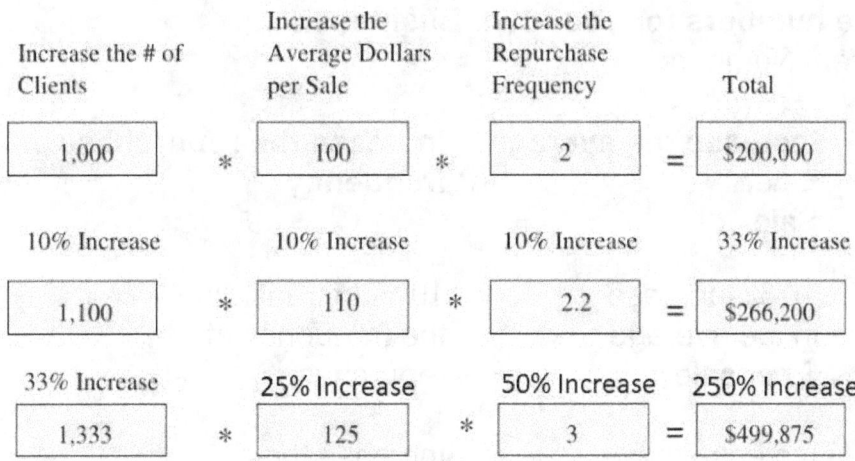

OPTIMIZATION

This illustration dramatizes the power of true geometry being harnessed for your business. Isn't this smarter than the strategy you're presently following?

5

LARGE COMPANY EXAMPLE:

| Current # of Customers

10.000 X | Increase the average £ per Sale
200 X | Increase the repurchase frequency
3 | Total

£6000.000 |
|---|---|---|---|
| 10 % increase | 10 % increase | 10 % increase | 33.1% |
| 20% increase | 20 increase | 20 %increase | 72.8 % |
| 33 % increase | 25% increase | 50 %increase | 150% |

51

Now fill out the numbers for your own Business:
PHASE 1: Current Numbers

Current # of Customers	Increase the average £ per Sale	Increase the repurchase frequency	Total
10 % Increase in the # of customers	10 % Increase in the average $ per sale	10 % Increase in the frequency of repurchase	Total
Increase the # of customers	Increase the average $ per sale	Increase the repurchase frequency	Total

JAY ABRAHAM'S "BUINESS PARTHENON":

To grow your client-base, you can focus on:
- Recommendation systems
- Delivering higher-than-expected levels of service
- Communicating frequently with your clients to nurture and make a profit on the back end.
- Advertising
- Increasing sales skills levels of your staff
- Running special events or information nights
- Increasing the perceived value of your product/service through a better client education.
- Guaranteeing purchases through risk reversal

"If you're attacking your market from multiple positions and your competitor isn't, you have all the advantage and it will show up in your increased success and income."

– JAY ABRAHAM

Notes:

PRINCIPLE 3

STRATEGIC INNOVATION AND EXPLOITING YOUR EXISTING BUSINESS

(The ability to reinvent the basics of competition within existing industries and invent entirely new industries)

"Innovation distinguishes between a leader and a follower."

- STEVE JOBS

4.1 Introduction:

Strategic innovation is one of the fundamental elements required to grow a successful business and it is redesigning its corporate strategy to drive business growth, generate value for the company and its customers and create a competitive advantage.

Nowadays, it is becoming more evident in our current marketplace. As we continue to develop new and more efficient technologies, the demand for improved innovation is increasing as well.

Consequently, being able to continually develop and integrate new ideas is becoming more and more important in today's business world. If you want to stay ahead, you've got to be in touch with not only your current customer needs, but your future customer demands, as well.

Master innovators are Sony, Coca-Cola, Apple, Starbucks, Google and so on.

4.2 Some keys to strategic innovation:

You have to start thinking as you get out of your "box" and shift your way of thinking. For example, how you can start to figure out what people need that they don't even know they need yet. You must change the rules of your industry and make it even more customized to your client's ultimate needs.

Here are three keys to help you stay ahead.

1. Be just ahead of the trend.
2. Ensure that there are infinite upsides.

3. Employ these 5 steps to innovate a company;

a) New Voices.

b) New Questions/New Conversations.

c) New Perspectives.

d) New Passions.

e) New Experiments

4.3 Strategy Innovation Exercise:

Brainstorm some ideas for how you can strategically innovate your organization.

New Voices?

New Questions/New Conversations?

New Views?

New Passions?

Experiments?

Who is your customer, really?

What business are you really in?

Are you really successful?

What does your customer really need now and in the next 5 years?

What business are you really in?

Why are you really successful?

Notes:

PRINCIPLE 4

THE WORLD-CLASS SALES MASTERY
The power to influence: solve problems and Win!

(Influencing yourself is 80% of sale success, influencing the prospect is only 20%)

"Everyone lives by selling something."
- ROBERT LOUIS STEVENSON

5.1 Introduction:

Leaders are the Masters of Influence. Everyone has different thinking regarding sales people. They think of money-hungry, slimy and manipulative liars. However, sale is about influencing others and there is no greater power than to be able to move another to take action. True leaders are masters at the skill of influence.

5.2 Meeting Your 6 Human Needs:

To influence other people, you must know what influences them and must already be influenced. All human beings have the need for:

- Certainty
- Uncertainty
- Significance
- Connection
- Contribution
- Growth

THE 4 NEEDS OF PERSONALITY	THE 2 NEEDS OF THE SPIRIT
Need 1 (connection and love)	Need 5 (growth)
Need 2 (significance)	Need 6 (contribution)
Need 3 (certainty)	
Need 4 (uncertainty)	

People always find ways to meet these needs in negative, positive, and neutral ways. But every person discovers a way to meet them by hook or by crook.
Any action, emotion and activity that fulfils at least three needs at a high level becomes, in effect, an addiction. Also, people have positive, negative and neutral addictions.

There is always a way to fulfil a need; the skill lies in finding a sustainable way to fulfil it and doing so in a way that gives you more pleasure than pain.

5.3 The Power of Questions:

Humans are emotional beings. Therefore, when you want to change a person's state, you have to influence him. So, how to change someone's state - By changing their focus, which can be accomplished by questions you ask them. When you want to influence others and yourself, ask better questions. Problems are questions that have not been answered. There are 3 steps to problem-solving:

Step 1:

Describe the problem and request.

Describe with precision in 1 or 2 sentences, the problem and request.

Step 2

Provide a solution.

What are 3 cost-effective, intelligent and practical solutions?

Which one of 3 is your favorite?

What resources of time, money and energy could be required?

Step 3

Respond.

Accept, modify or reject, with a reason to provide new alternative solutions.

SAMPLE: Problem-Solving Questions

1. What can I learn from this?
2. What's great about this problem?
3. What is not perfect yet?
4. What am I willing to do to make it the way I want it?
5. What am I not willing to do to make it the way I want it?
6. How can I enjoy the process?

"It's in your moments of decision that your destiny is shaped."
- Tony Robbins

Notes:

PRINCIPLE 5

THE RAPID PLANNING METHOD

(3 Master Steps to take immediate control of your Time, Life and Business)

"The truth of the matter is that you always know the right thing to do. The hard part is doing it."
- NORMAN SCHWARZKOPF JR.

6.1 Create RPA Culture (Result Purpose Action):

Are you a **result manager** or an **activity manager**?

You must understand, as there is a huge difference between managing results and managing activities. As, in a business and life, what you focus on in business is what you get. In order to align a group of diverse individuals with different mindsets and values to produce measurable results, forget the best outcome. You must learn to focus on people for a common outcome or result. For example, in Desert Storm, General Norman Schwarzkopf was able to do this with allied forces composed of soldiers from many different religious beliefs, different nations, races and politics. When he noticed that people started to focus on their differences, he simply kept bringing it back to their one core outcome: to kick Saddam Hussain out of Kuwait. In many businesses, managers focus on activities instead of results. As a result, with managing activities, you can accomplish all your to-dos and get all the activities done but do not really achieve anything valuable for your customers and meaningful for business.

You must remember - most of the businesses identify their purpose to be one of two things: to define a set of core values or transform the quality of life for their customers and to make a profit by having a business that is result-focused and purpose-driven. For that, you have to create an opportunity to fulfil this mission while altogether giving the people who work there, the ability to find meaning in what they do.

The **most powerful planning method** and a very simple one is called **RPA – Result, Purpose, Action plan**. It provides the solution for taking all of the massive amounts of information, activities, requests, inputs, phone calls and demands and so on and bringing them into a focus that produces measurable results. With this method, you can consistently achieve amazing results.

6.2 How can you turn your Dreams, Goals and Desires into Reality?

The RPA Management System is a proven system for taking anything you can visualize and making it real and with this, you can learn not only how to organize but you can also learn how to think differently from those who become muddled in an ocean of activities.

RESULT:

First, it teaches you how to ask the most important questions that all people who succeed ask.

What do I want from this situation?

What is my outcome?

What is my result?

What should I do?

What is the result I am committed to achieving?

After you answer these questions, you can be absolutely clear about what you exactly want (your desired result) and any to-do list you create will be generalized and effective.

PURPOSE

Secondly, you find out and you must know why you are doing and what you are doing. When you know the purpose, the P in RPA, having a sense of real purpose compelling reasons will provide you with the necessary drive to make this result or outcome a reality.

You need to remember that there is a huge difference between having reasons to push yourself through the inevitable obstacles, simply by having a dream and thereby achieving a worthwhile goal. You can find many ways to achieve a result, but you must have the necessary drive to follow through and you must know why you are going after it.

ACTION PLAN

Finally, when you know the exact result you are committed to achieving, for example, why you must achieve it (the purpose), what it will give you physically, psychologically and emotionally. Now you are in the state of mind to begin creating an action plan by asking yourself what you must do in order to achieve this precise result.

The difference between success and failure. The order in which you determine these three elements is knowing:

What you want?

Why you want it?

How you will achieve it?

6.3 The Power of Mastering RPA:

Individuals who succeed always start with the end in the mind - they are totally clear about the final result they are after. They have unleashed the power of why. They have a burning desire to achieve their results, and it is tied to a specific and clear goal. Creating the action plan is simply when these first two elements are put together. When you have developed results – focused, purpose-driven and a massive action plan for your week, your day or your month or for any project or goal that you are committed to achieving, you will have created the certainty of knowing.

6.4 How to create an extraordinary quality of life with the RPA method:

This system taps the power of focus.

What you consistently focus on will be achieved. The RPA Management System causes you to focus on the result you are committed to, with complete focus on the result. You will be able to come up with a more effective action plan. If your plan does not work, you will find another way to achieve what you are after.

The RPA Management System taps the power of anticipation.

With traditional to-do planning, the question asked is: "What do I need to do today or this week?" As we already stated in the RPA process, one asks:
- What are the most important results that I need to achieve?
- Why do I want to accomplish these tasks and what will it give me?
- What actions must I take in order to achieve this result?

RPA planning taps the power of synergy.

In traditional to-do list planning, one does not take any time to note the relationships between tasks. Therefore, the opportunity to accomplish multiple tasks at the same time or to maximize your effectiveness in a
given situation by combining tasks is missed.

6.5 The Power of Chunking:

It refers to grouping together information into ideally sized pieces so that they can be used effectively to produce the results that you want without being stressed or overwhelmed. Its power is well-known to those who have tried and mastered it.

6.6 Wheel of Life Exercise (Created by Paul J. Meyer):

Directions: The eight sections in the Wheel of Life represent balance. Considering the center of the wheel as 0 and the outer edge as 10, rank your level of satisfaction with each life area by drawing a straight or curved line to create a new outer edge (see example below). The new perimeter of the circle represents the Wheel of Life. How bumpy would the ride be if this was a real wheel?

WHEEL OF LIFE EXERCISE

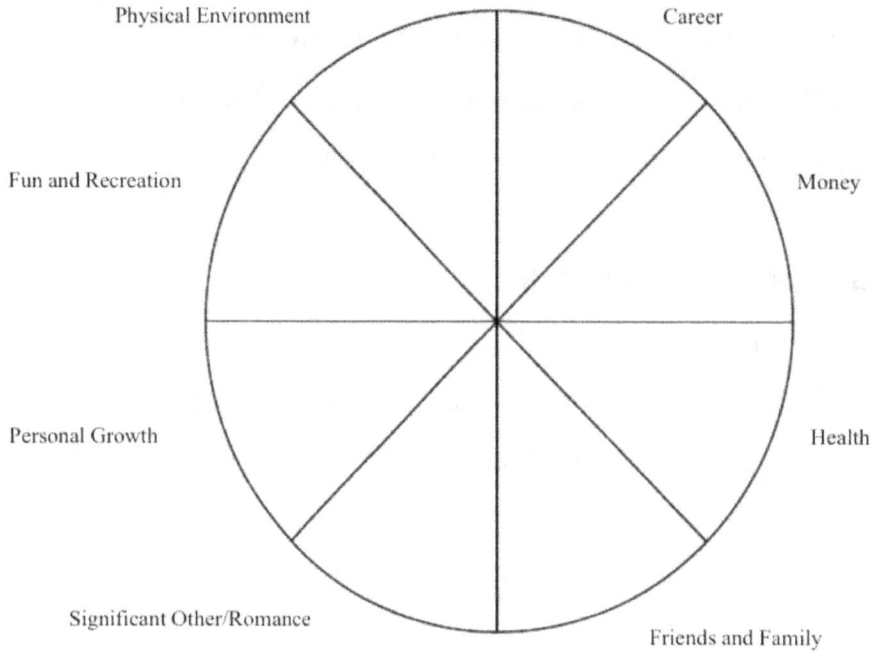

Wheel of Life Exercise

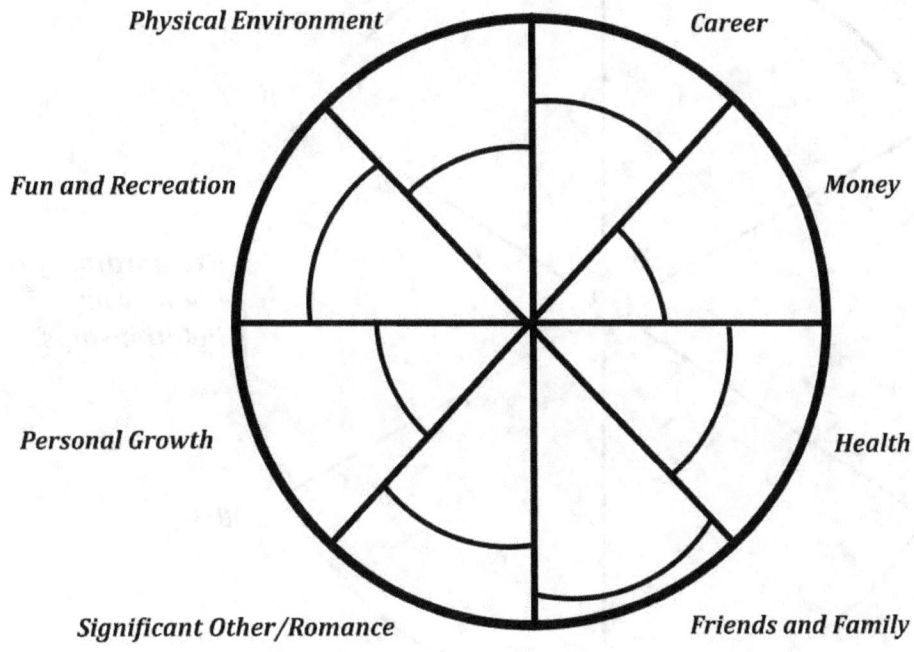

If this was a tyre on your car called life, how would the car run?

What if you were going 30mph?

What if you were an achiever going 100mph?

6.7 Now take a look at your Professional Life:

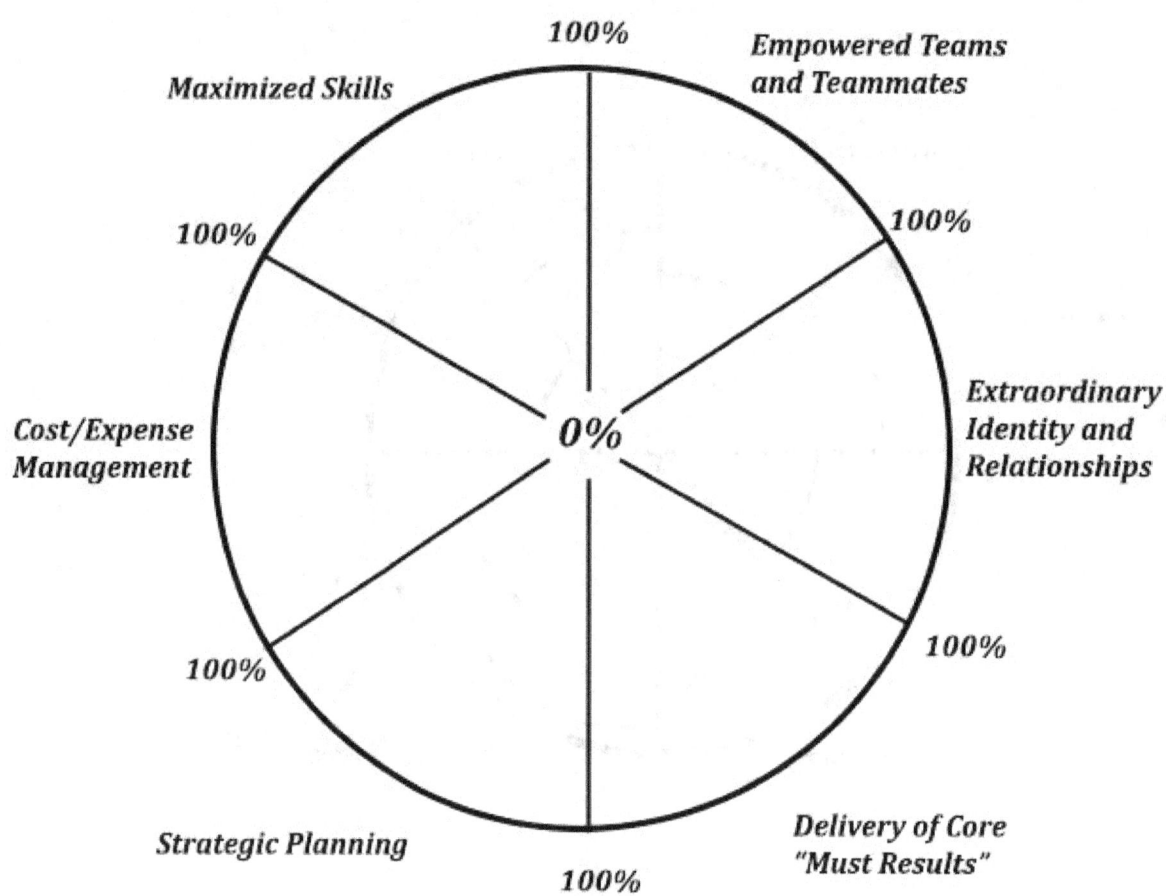

6.8 Wheel of Your Business:

Directions: The eight sections in the Wheel of Life measure and manage the health of your organization balance. Regarding the center of the wheel as 0 and the outer edge as 10, rank your level of satisfaction with each life area by drawing a straight or curved line to create a new outer edge (see example below). The new perimeter of the circle represents the Wheel of Life. How bumpy would the ride be if this was a real wheel?

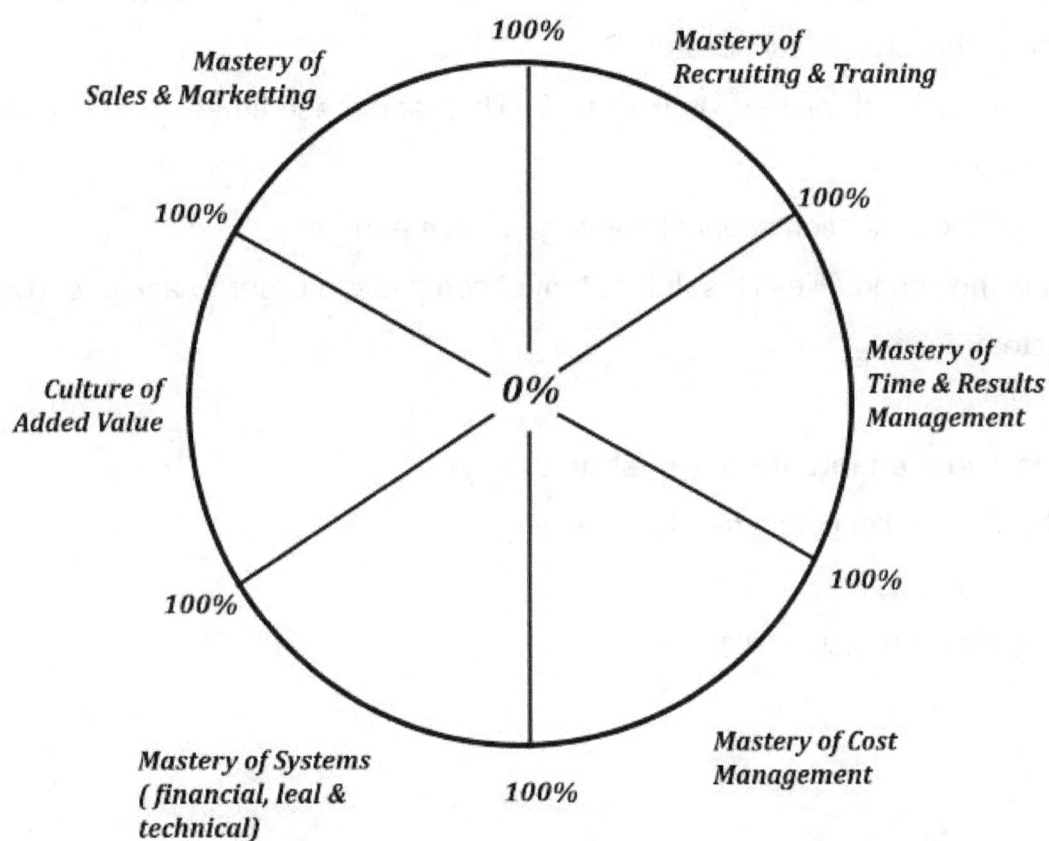

6.9 Using RPA for your project:

RESULT (What is the ultimate outcome that I need to achieve? What is the result I want to produce?)

Purpose (Why do I want to do this? What is my ultimate purpose for completing the project? What will it give me if I achieve this? How will this make me feel?)

Map or action plan:
- What are the most important outcomes/results I must produce in order to complete this project successfully?
- How long will each of these items take? (Then add these times up to find out the duration)
- Which of these sections could I leverage to someone else?
- What is the second Key Result that I must complete in order to achieve my ultimate outcome?

Even RPA is chunked into three questions for you:
1) What is the Result I'm committed to achieving?
2) What is my Purpose?
3) What is my Massive Action Plan?

Notes:

PRINCIPLE 6
THE ULTIMATE SUCCESS FORMULA FOR MAKING YOUR BUSINESS SUCCESSFUL

(You will discover your business' X-Factor, create a core story, discover how to hire and keep superstars and find a precise strategy for your business)

"Entrepreneurship - The act that endows resources with a new capacity to create wealth."

- PETER DRUCKER

7.1 The ULTIMATE SUCCESS FORMULA for making your business successful:

When you want to create a business in which you can find more enjoyment and fulfilment, the **secret to unstoppable success** is in mastering the little things that can make a giant difference. Also, you want to really change your business and take it to an entirely new level of growth, competitive edge, and profitability.

7.2 The X-Factor (The Success Factor: Unconventional Wisdom for Business Success)

X-Factor, according to Ernane Lung, is in the business' ability to find a way to do more for your customers than anybody else and to consistently maintain that standard. It is the ability to find a way to add intangible value - value that goes beyond what anybody can really measure.

Besides, what is your vision and a way of gaining clarity around your outcomes, what business you are in and what you can bring to the marketplace. It can be your culture, your mission or something else, small but meaningful. Understand the thinking of your ideal customer, where and how to find them, and how to market in a way that attracts customers you want, while repelling those you don't want. You'll learn to do more of the things you love doing, and less of the things you hate doing.

Some companies are continually bringing forward a dynamic fusion of new ideas in art and technology. For example, Apple Computer has dominated the telecommunications, music, and computer industries.

Amazon has become the go-to for ordering just about anything online because of their expedited shipping through Prime. Their X-Factor is their prime membership. Their X-Factor is a constant innovation.

Leadership with deliberate regard of the X-factor is, who you are and what you bring to the marketplace instead of what everyone else is bringing in the market. Bring the good stuff and increase your profit. Your X-factor could be your finances and being able to see how and where you can really make a difference. It can be an ability to influence people, and about making strategic decisions. It can be a vision or a way of gaining clarity around your outcomes

The following companies are some of the most successful businesses:

Apple	Johnson & Johnson
Google	Oracle
Volkswagen	LG Electronics
Amazon	Walmart Stores
Hewlett-Packard (HP)	General Electronic
Microsoft	Hyundai Motors
JP Morgan & Chase Co.	Procter & Gamble
Dell	Exxon Mobile
IBM	Samsung Electronics
Coca-Cola	Chevron

7.3 Find out the X-Factor in your business (the ultimate competitive advantage):

The X-Factor is really a leader's ability to improve the quality of life and experience for their customers – both internally and externally. And maximize resources in a way that gets the outcome of creating business breakthroughs that maximize value using a combination of skills, psychology and experience to find that edge that makes a difference for your customers in their life.

7.4 EXERCISE:

Every business has its own X-Factor. Your business' X-Factor could be financial analysis and could be your culture. It may be your mission. It could be negotiation or any distinction you make that could change it all.

For generating an X-Factor in your business, it requires a combination of skills, psychology and experience to find your competitive edge. For that, honestly answer the following questions:

1. What makes your company stand out?

_____
_____
_____
_____
_____

2. What offers your customers the most value?

_____
_____

_____

_____

_____

3. What is your company great at?

_____

_____

_____

_____

4. What makes you stand out individually?

_____

_____

_____

_____

_____

5. What will your X Factor become?

_____

_____

_____

_____

_____

7.5 What is the X-Factor in your business?

Two parts you should be working on:
1) Which business you or the company you are in

- Don't take your eyes off the ball
- Day-to-day business and everyday improvements

2) The company you are going to become

If you don't talk about this, you will become the company you were.

EXERCISE:

What are some of the biggest risks in your organization? Write down your risks and then brainstorm a solution for each one.

Risk:
_____
_____
_____

Solution:
_____
_____
_____

Risk:
_____
_____
_____

Solution:

_____

_____

Risk:

_____

_____

Solution:

_____

_____

7.6 What is the X-Factor in your business?

(Triggers for Failure and Triggers for Growth)

In any business, there are triggers that lead to failure or growth.

Exercise: Think about some of the biggest failures in your company. What were the triggers that caused you to fail?

_____

_____

_____

_____

_____

_____

_____

Exercise: Think about the time when you had the biggest successes in your company. What are some triggers that have led to growth in the past?

_____
_____
_____
_____
_____
_____
_____

7.7 FIND OUT YOUR PERSONAL X- FACTOR

Rate yourself on a scale of 1 to 10, circle the top 3 that are affecting your business the most:

SKILLS	SCALE OF 1 TO 10:
Marketing	1 2 3 4 5 6 7 8 9 10
Innovation/Creation	1 2 3 4 5 6 7 8 9 10
Leadership/Influence	1 2 3 4 5 6 7 8 9 10
Culture	1 2 3 4 5 6 7 8 9 10
Decision making/execution	1 2 3 4 5 6 7 8 9 10
Optimization	1 2 3 4 5 6 7 8 9 10
Sales	1 2 3 4 5 6 7 8 9 10
Financial Intelligence	1 2 3 4 5 6 7 8 9 10
Ability to Identify & Keep Key Talent	1 2 3 4 5 6 7 8 9 10

Exercise: What standards and habits do you have that make you stand out from the rest?

It could be an added value and surpassing the client's expectations every time and the hunger to serve.

_____
_____
_____
_____
_____
_____

Exercise: What experience and skills do you have that give you X-Factor?

_____
_____
_____
_____
_____
_____

Exercise: What experiences and skills are missing in you?

_____
_____
_____
_____
_____
_____

7.8 Find out your personal X-Factor:

One X-Factor in your business ID is you.

STRENGTHS	WEAKNESSES

Exercise:

Have you thought about how you are going to resolve these weaknesses?

How can you be specific?

_____
_____
_____
_____

What new skills and strategies are you committed to mastering?

_____
_____
_____
_____
_____

What system will you put in place?

_____
_____
_____
_____
_____

Who will you hire? Who would manage them?

_____
_____
_____
_____
_____

Finding the X-Factor in your business is your opportunity to stand out. Where you are weak, you will need to find ways to get strong and innovate new solutions, create raving fan customers and continually add extraordinary value to your customers. This will keep you ahead of the game and earn significant profits for years to come. However, if you are going to be the leader, you may not be able to do it all, but you've got to be able to lead it all.

7.9 Change your Limiting Beliefs which stop your growth:

When you believe something is impossible, you only see what is stopping you. But when you start to believe that something can happen, you notice new possibilities and opportunities.

Exercise:

1) Identify three limiting beliefs that have been producing limiting beliefs with unwanted or negative consequences in your business?

_____
_____
_____
_____
_____
_____
_____
_____
_____
_____

2) What negative consequences have you already experienced because of this belief?

_____
_____
_____
_____

3) Now make a list of at least five positive beliefs that can now serve to support you in achieving the highest success in your business?

_____
_____
_____
_____
_____

Notes:

PRINCIPLE 7

CREATING FAN CUSTOMERS AND IDEAS TO GET NEW CUSTOMERS

(Consistently add more value and give your customers what they want)

"There is only one boss – The customer. And he can fire everybody in the company, simply by spending his money somewhere else."
- SAM WALTON

8.1 Introduction:

COMMIT to your business. Believe in it more than anybody else does. If you love your work or business, you'll be out there every day trying to give the best you possibly can. But what one thing you would adapt and see it as an organization that would create an immediate and huge change in the quality and profitability of your business. Have you thought what it would be?

Sam Walton's Philosophy of Success (you must understand): "Anticipate and consistently fulfil the deepest needs of your clients and give your customers what they want."

This is really the core strategy behind the best organizations. Any organization which wants to create a long-term success must have an extremely high customer loyalty and they must fulfil their client's needs to the highest level.
According to Jim Rohn," One customer, well-taken care of, could be more valuable than $10.000 worth of advertising". You already know, the most expensive thing you can do as a business is to acquire a new customer - it takes most of your money, energy and time. In any organization, it is the hardest thing that they do. So, the simple way to make additional money is to continually serve that same customer. But there is a challenge and it is that if you hold them as a customer, you have only a temporary nature of relationship.

For keeping the same customer, your organizational goals should be to create quality clients. When you have clients, it changes your role from someone who's trying to give something, so you get something back to the role of a fiduciary (involving trust), where it's your responsibility to do what's in the best interest of the client.

> **The biggest mistake most organizations make:**
> They fall in love with their business and products but they do not fall in love with their clients.

8.2 Do you love your clients or customers?

"One of the biggest mistakes, probably the biggest mistake, people make in any business is that they fall in love with the wrong things. They fall in love with their product, service or company. You should believe passionately in your product, service or company. But you should fall in love with your clients." Jay Abraham, Getting All You Can Out of All You've Got.

When you want to keep your customers, there is a very simple marketing technique that is more effective than attracting customers. That is with a genuine and sincere concern, coupled with a true desire to assist them in solving their problems and fulfil their deepest needs.

For example, you goal is not only to understand this intellectually, but also to appreciate it emphatically, where you can literally feel what's going on with them. You are able to create a level of relationship where you know more about your clients' needs, goals, wounds and desires than they know themselves.
In your organization, when you generate more strategic philosophy, where you are not just looking to make the sale, but rather to create a long-term relationship where you look out for your client's best interest at all times, the more your organization is going to transform.

8.3 How to Build Relationship with your clients:

Although we all have the same 6 human needs, we value them in different proportions. **Step two** is to learn what your customers' top needs are, what has happened to them and why they want to experience those needs.

Your business needs to be based not on the product, but on the customer with love, worship, caring, understanding and empathy where you are constantly finding a better way to meet their needs.

THE 6 HUMAN NEEDS:

1. **Certainty**: assurance, you can avoid pain and gain pleasure
2. **Uncertainty/Variety**: the need for the unknown, change and new stimuli
3. **Significance**: feeling unique, important, special or needed
4. **Connection/Love**: a strong feeling of closeness
5. **Growth**: an expansion of capacity, capability or understanding
6. **Contribution**: a sense of service and focus on helping, giving and supporting others.

EXERCISE:

Which of these needs does your customer value the most? Which needs come in the second place?

_____
_____
_____
_____

What has to happen for your customers to feel that their needs are being met?

_____
_____
_____
_____

Can you think of some other more creative and innovating ways for meeting those needs? Be creative – think of three or more ways to meet your customer's top two needs.

_____
_____
_____
_____

> Your goal should always be to leverage your relationship with the client to its maximum benefit, result and mutual value.

8.4 Keys for Creating Raving Fan Clients:

When you are totally focused on your product, you may overlook what's best for your client and your product is nothing without a client to sell it to. However, a happy client creates a great product as when your client is your number one priority, your product becomes tailored to their interests.

Regularly Create Raving Fan Clients and Culture. It is not just about being different; it provides so much value that your clients can't help but tell others about it — with a genuine enthusiasm and excitement.

When you want to Create Raving Fan Clients and Culture, you have to understand, anticipate and consistently fulfill the deepest needs of your clients. To do this, you must live by some of these commandments.

1. You need to give more than you promote and put the customer first. Don't wait for opportunities to present themselves. Seek them out. Give customers more than they expect. Also, you need to provide incredible service to create clients for life because happy and satisfied customers are the lifeblood of any successful business.
2. You can reward your best customers by giving them special benefits, discounts, offers and value in addition to what your core clients are receiving.
3. You always leave your client in a better place and always be available for them. For example, people are not buying products; they are buying the pleasure they get from products. You must keep everything in your power to help your clients get the results they desire from your products. Also, make sure your customers know you are available on demand. Be involved in the same social media channels as your customers.
4. You can create unexpected surprises and bonuses. As customers love surprises – but only when they are good surprises. Your job is to create those positive surprises that will excite and delight customers. For example: High-class – your surprise should be a special gift for the customer that non-customers don't get

   Relevant – your surprise should be a good match, companion, or accessory to the main purchase.

   Start with a small but needed gift. Try surprising customers in a good way (for once) and you'll be amazed at how they return to do business with you again. If your surprise is good enough, they may even tell some friends.

5. You must run your business in an open and a transparent way. For example, when something goes wrong, tell your clients what happened. When you make your offers, be totally clear what it means to your clients.
6. In your business structure and system, you must create space that allow everyone in your company to consistently meet your client's needs. For example: keeping up with the market, planning ahead, cash flow and financial management, problem solving, the right systems and skills and attitudes. Also, business is the management of promises; consistent delivery (or exceeding) of promises fulfilled to your internal and external customers.
7. Outstanding client support and service is affected by every person in your organization - from the receptionist to the mailroom clerk to CEO. You must create a culture where people are passionate about meeting the client's needs.
8. You must periodically question conventional wisdom about what you think your customers need and want. Remember Henry Ford: If I would have asked my customers what they wanted; they would have said a faster horse.

8.5 How to Increase Your Number of Clients:

1) Recommendation systems.
2) Acquiring customers at break-even upfront and make a profit on the back-end.
3) Guaranteeing purchases through risk reversals.
4) Host/beneficiary relationships.
5) Advertising.
6) Using direct mail.
7) Using telemarketing.
8) Running special events or information nights
9) Acquiring qualified lists.

10) Develop a Unique Selling Proposition.

11) Increasing the perceived value of your product or service through better customer education.

12) Using public relations.

13) Sequential Integrated Internet, Website & Email

How to Increase Transaction Frequency?

1) Developing a back-end of products that you can go back to your customers with.

2) Communicating personally with your customers to maintain a positive relationship.

3) Endorsing other people's products to your list.

4) Running special events such as "closed door sales," limited pre-releases, etc.

5) Pre-framing or programming customers in advance.

6) Price inducements for frequency of purchases.

8.6 Summary:

I have known which distinctions and strategies the key success and income-increasing principles in business are. They are most powerful, most enduring, most universally applicable and most effective strategies for building your business massively. That will save your time, money and opportunity costs. It enables you to run rings around all of your competitors, before they ever figure out what you did to them. And it virtually guarantees you greater success and multiplied profits from every business-building step you ever take.

You are about to begin a wonderful and exciting journey. Embrace these strategies, apply them with diligence and your final destination will be financial security, distinction, recognition and much deserved success. I wish you the best of success in all your entrepreneurial and business endeavors.

Notes:

CONGRATULATIONS

Wow! You have completed the Business Expertise course successfully. I am sure it will help generate leadership skills within you and help master the already existing skills.

References:

1. Dias, C. and Abraham, J. Find the Motherlode of Wealth in Your Business. 2013.
2. Robbins, A. Unlimited power. Simon & Schuster Paperbacks, New York, 2015.
3. Schwarzkopf, H. and Petre, P. General H. Norman Schwarzkopf. Bantam, London, 1992.
4. Meyer, P. I inherited a fortune!. Legacy Books, Arlington, Tex., 1997.
5. Meyer, P. Personal Motivation. Originally published, 2005.
6. Richard Reck, R. The X-Factor: Getting Extraordinary Results from Ordinary People. 2001.
7. Heil, G., Stephens, D. and Bennis, W. Douglas McGregor, revisited. Wiley, New York, 2000.
8. Lung, E. The Success Factor: Unconventional Wisdom for Small Business Success. Morgan James Publishing, 2017.
9. Apple. Apple, 2019. https://www.apple.com/
10. Amazon.com: Online Shopping for Electronics, Apparel, Computers, Books, DVDs & more. Amazon.com, 2019. https://www.amazon.com/
11. The ultimate sales machine - chet holmes. Primento Digital, [United States], 2
12. Bandler, R. Get the life you want. HarperCollins, London, 2009..
13. Bandler, R., Roberti, A. and Fitzpatrick, O. The ultimate introduction to NLP. HarperCollins Publishers, London, 2013.

14. Robbins, A. (2015). Unlimited power. New York: Simon & Schuster Paperbacks.
15. Abraham, J. Getting Everything You Can Out of All You've Got. 2011.
16. Abraham, J. (2013). Getting everything you can out of all you've got. New York:

St. Martin's Press.

17. Abraham, J. (2009). The Sticking Point Solution: 9 Ways to Move Your Business from Stagnation to Stunning Growth in Tough Economic Times. vanguard press.

18. Ilgen, D. and Pulakos, E. (1999). The changing nature of performance. San Francisco: Jossey-Bass Publishers.

19. Robbins, T. (2015). Tony Robbins: 25 Business Lessons of Tony Robbins and How to Make Your Business Plan (Tony Robbins, money, investing, business, business tools, ... self motivation, make money) (Volume 2).

20. Publishing, B. (2015). Summary. Cork: Primento Digital.

21. Hallman, S. (2018). The 7 success drivers to hypergrowth. united states of America.

22. Mohamed, N. (2017). Financial socialization: a cornerstone for young employees' financial well-being. Reports on Economics and Finance, 3, pp.15-35.

23. Abraham, J. (2013). Find the Motherlode of Wealth in Your Business Hardcover. executive learning systgems, inc.

24. Forbes.com (2019). [online] Available at: https://www.forbes.com/2003/01/13/cz_rb_0113kinkos.html [Accessed 8 Apr. 2019].

25. Taylor, Harriet (August 30, 2016). "How Apple managed to pay such a low tax rate in Ireland". CNBC. Retrieved January 9, 2017.

26. Rice, Valerie (April 15, 1985). "Unrecognized Apple II Employees Exit". InfoWorld. p. 35. Retrieved November 6, 2017.

27. Schwind, H. (1978). An Alternative to Behaviorally Anchored Rating Scales: The Behavior Description Index. Academy of Management Proceedings, 1978(1), pp.38-42.

28. Singh, T. and Behera, M. (2016). Application of the Maslow's Hierarchy of Need

Theory: Impacts and Implications on Employee's Career Stages. Training & Development Journal, 7(2), p.43.

29. Wu, W. (2012). The Relationship between Incentives to Learn and Maslow's Hierarchy of Needs. Physics Procedia, 24, pp.1335-1342.

30. Zvavahera (PhD), P. and Tandi, R. (2019). Application and implications of Maslow's Hierarchy of Needs Theory: The Zimbabwean experience. Turk Turizm Arastirmalari Dergisi, 2(3), pp.63-82.

31. Citigroup.com. (2019). [online] Available at: https://www.citigroup.com/citi/citizen/community/data/guide10_eng.pdf [Accessed 8 Apr. 2019].

32. Rock-Evans, R. (2014). Analysis within the Systems Development Life-Cycle: Data Analysis. Elsevier Science.

33. Gilkey, C. (2014). The small business life cycle.

34. Carter, M. (2013). Life Cycle Analysis. Mark James Carter.

35. Austrian, s. (2008). Developmental Theories Through the Life Cycle. 2nd ed. New York Chichester, West Sussex: Columbia University Press.

36. Rockefeller., J. (2017). Sam Walton - His Life and His Philosophy.

37. Rockefeller., J. (2016). Sam Walton: Inspirational Story (Walmart) and Tips for Success.

38. Bandler, R., Roberti, A. and Fitzpatrick, O. (2013). The ultimate introduction to NLP. London: HarperCollins Publisher

www.ingramcontent.com/pod-product-compliance
Lightning Source LLC
Chambersburg PA
CBHW080554220526
45466CB00010B/3151